This book belongs to

....

The Beehive Fence
and Other Stories

How this collection works

This *Biff, Chip and Kipper* collection is one of a series of four books at **Read with Oxford Stage 5**. It contains four stories: *The Beehive Fence, A Good Turn, What a Journey!* and *The Fair-Haired Samurai*. These stories will help to broaden your child's wider reading experience. There are also fun activities to enjoy throughout the book.

How to use this book

Find a time to read with your child when they are not too tired and are happy to concentrate for about fifteen to twenty minutes, or longer if they are enjoying the story. Reading with your child should be a shared and enjoyable experience. It is best to choose just one of the stories for each session.

For each story, there are tips for reading the story together. At the end of each story you will find four 'Talk about the story' questions. These will help your child to think about what they have read, and to relate the story to their own experiences. The questions are followed by a fun activity.

Enjoy sharing the stories!

Contents

The Beehive Fence   5

A Good Turn   41

What a Journey!   77

The Fair-Haired Samurai 113

OXFORD

UNIVERSITY PRESS

Authors and illustrators

The Beehive Fence written by Roderick Hunt, illustrated by Alex Brychta

A Good Turn written by Roderick Hunt, illustrated by Alex Brychta

What a Journey! written by Roderick Hunt, illustrated by Alex Brychta

The Fair-haired Samurai written by Roderick Hunt, illustrated by Alex Brychta

OXFORD
UNIVERSITY PRESS

Great Clarendon Street, Oxford, OX2 6DP, United Kingdom

Oxford University Press is a department of the University
of Oxford. It furthers the University's objective of excellence
in research, scholarship, and education by publishing
worldwide. Oxford is a registered trade mark of Oxford
University Press in the UK and in certain other countries

The Beehive Fence, A Good Turn, What a Journey!, The Fair-haired Samurai
text © Roderick Hunt 2015

The Beehive Fence, A Good Turn, What a Journey!, The Fair-haired Samurai
illustrations © Alex Brychta 2015

The characters in this work are the original creation of Roderick Hunt
and Alex Brychta who retain copyright in the characters

The moral rights of the author have been asserted

The Beehive Fence, A Good Turn, What a Journey!, The Fair-haired Samurai
first published in 2015

This Edition published in 2018

British Library Cataloguing in Publication Data
Data available

ISBN: 978-0-19-276431-7

10 9 8 7 6 5

Paper used in the production of this book is a natural, recyclable product
made from wood grown in sustainable forests. The manufacturing process
conforms to the environmental regulations of the country of origin.

Printed in Great Britain by Bell and Bain Ltd, Glasgow

Acknowledgements

Series editor: Annemarie Young

Additional artwork by Nick Schon

MIX
Paper from
responsible sources
FSC
www.fsc.org FSC® C007785

Tips for reading *The Beehive Fence*

Children learn best when reading is relaxed and enjoyable.

- Talk about the title and the picture on page 6.
  Then read the speech bubble.

- Discuss what you think the story might be about.

- Encourage your child to read as much of the story as they can.

- Give lots of praise as your child reads, and help them
  when necessary.

- If your child gets stuck on a word that is decodable, encourage
  them to say the sounds and then blend them together to read the
  word. Read the whole sentence again. Focus on the meaning.

- If the word is not decodable, or is still too tricky, just read the
  word for them, re-read the sentence and move on.

- Where you can, use voices for different characters. Encourage
  your child to do the same. Reading with expression is fun.

- When you've finished reading the story, talk about it with your
  child, using the 'Talk about the story' questions at the end.
  Then do the activity.

Children enjoy re-reading stories, and this helps to build
their confidence.

Have fun!

For more activities, free eBooks
and practical advice to help
your child progress with reading
visit **oxfordowl.co.uk**

The Beehive Fence

Will Biff overcome her fear of bees to help some villagers in Africa to protect their crops?

Anneena had come for a sleepover with Biff. It was a warm summer evening and Biff had a good idea.

"Could Anneena and I sleep outside in the tent tonight?" she asked. "We'll put it up."

"All right," said Mum. "You may."

The girls were putting sleeping bags in the tent when Biff began to flap her arms. "Dad! Dad! There's a bee in the tent."

Biff began to swing her pillow at the bee.

"Hey!" cried Anneena. "Stop it! Keep still! Let me shoo it out."

When everything was set up, Biff and Anneena went indoors and made a picnic.

They brought out drinks and sandwiches for all the family. It wasn't long before bees began to buzz round the food.

"Oh no!" exclaimed Biff. "More bees!"

Suddenly there were hundreds of bees flying into the garden.

"It's a swarm," said Dad. "We'd better go inside."

Biff began to panic.

"Oh! Oh!" said Biff. "What if they fly into my hair?"

"They won't," said Anneena. "All the bees are following the queen bee. Once she settles somewhere all the bees will cluster together."

The bees began to form into a big ball on a branch of the apple tree.

"That's amazing," said Chip. "But what happens to the swarm now it has settled?"

"I'll phone my dad," said Anneena.

Anneena's dad kept bees so he knew what to do. He had his beekeeper's suit and a large box.

"They are honey bees," he said. "I'll take the swarm away and put it into a hive. Anneena can help me."

Anneena put on her bee suit, too. She held the box while her dad carefully eased the swarm into it.

Biff watched through the kitchen window.

"Now I see why Anneena knows so much about bees," she thought.

Before he went, Anneena's dad spoke to Biff.

"You must not be scared of bees," he said. "They are really useful. They carry pollen from one plant to another to help them produce crops. A lot of the food we eat is thanks to bees."

"I'll try not to be scared," said Biff.

Later on, Anneena was in the tent and Biff went to her room to get a book.

Anneena's bee suit was lying on Biff's bed so, for a joke, she put the suit on.

"This will make Anneena laugh," she thought. "Me wearing her bee suit!"

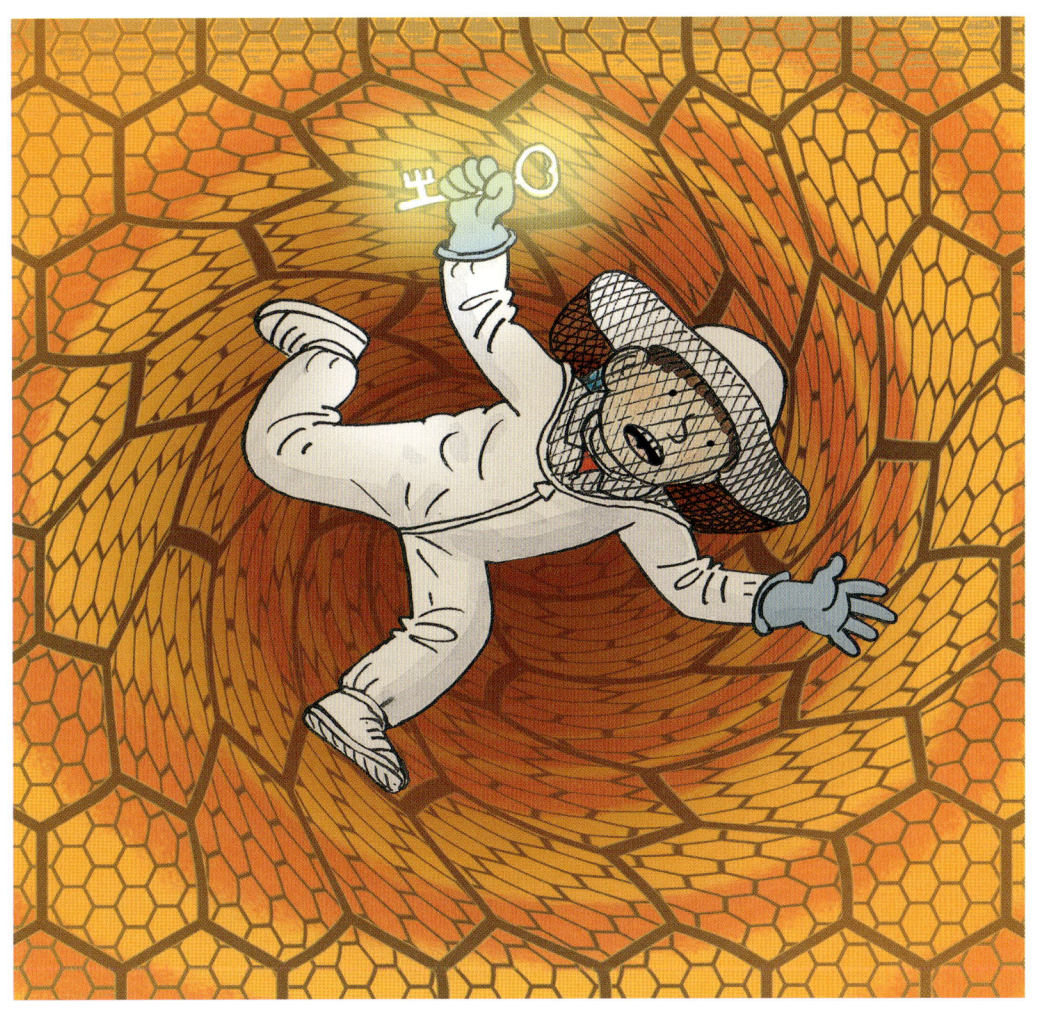

At that moment the key began to glow.

"Oh no!" cried Biff. "I don't want an adventure now. Not in this bee suit. It's sure to involve bees!"

But the key whisked her away.

The key took Biff to Kenya in Africa. In front of
her was a village. She felt very odd in the bee suit. She
wondered why the key had brought her here.

A boy and girl were coming towards her.

When they saw Biff, they stopped. The girl set down her basket.

"I am Karani," the boy said excitedly, "and this is my sister Mukami. Have you brought the bees for us?"

Before Biff had time to pull the hood off the bee suit, the boy and girl ran towards the first house.

"Babu! Babu! The bee lady is here!" they shouted.

"What can they mean?" thought Biff.

An elderly man came out of the house. Soon, other people from the village crowded round Biff.

Babu looked at Biff.

"You look very young to be the bee lady," he said. "Do you have the hives?"

Biff was confused. This was a strange adventure. She had no idea what to do or what to say.

"Do you mean beehives?" she asked.

"They raided our crops again last night," said Mukami. "They did such damage."

"We tried to keep the raiders out with sharp thorny branches, but that hasn't stopped them," said Babu. "And we are afraid of them when they are all together."

"They trample or eat our crops of sweet potatoes and cabbages," said Mukami.

"When they came last night," went on Babu, "we just shut our doors and hoped they would go away. That is why we need the hives. They are afraid of bees."

Everyone looked eagerly at Biff.

"We have made frames to hang the hives on," a man said. "So where are the bees?"

Biff opened her mouth and shut it again. She had no bees. She didn't know why bees would keep raiders away.

A truck drove up. A woman jumped out.

"Sorry I'm late," she said. "My truck broke down and I had to borrow this one. But I have the hives at last."

"We are so glad you are here," said Babu. "Your assistant came some time ago."

The woman looked at Biff in surprise.

"I didn't expect someone so young," she said. "Well! Let's get the hives set up."

Biff gasped in surprise. Not long ago, she had been afraid of a single bee. Now she was about to help set up beehives!

"My name is Mama Johari," the woman said to Biff. "Come on! We must work fast. It will be dark soon. Help me unload the truck."

The beehives were long wooden boxes. These had to be hung on the frames that the villagers had made.

Biff helped Mama Johari carry the beehives to the
frames and tie them on. Some bees flew out and buzzed
round Biff's hood. But she was too busy to mind.

Soon there was a beehive fence all round the
villagers' fields.

The sun went down and it grew dark. From not far off, came a deep trumpeting sound. It was the call of elephants!

"They are coming!" breathed Mukami.

Biff was astonished. Could the raiders be elephants? And were they afraid of bees?

Then, out of the darkness, Biff could hear them!
A whole herd of elephants!

Mama Johari handed Biff her night-vision
binoculars. Biff looked through them and gasped.

The elephants had reached the bee fence. They were led by a large female. Behind her came a large group of female elephants and two young ones. They stopped, as if unsure of something.

"What a sight!" breathed Biff.

Mama Johari had fixed a wire between the beehives, joining them all together.

The large female flapped her ears. She sensed the wire was there and, for a moment, she stood quite still.

"Let's see if she moves closer," said Mama Johari.

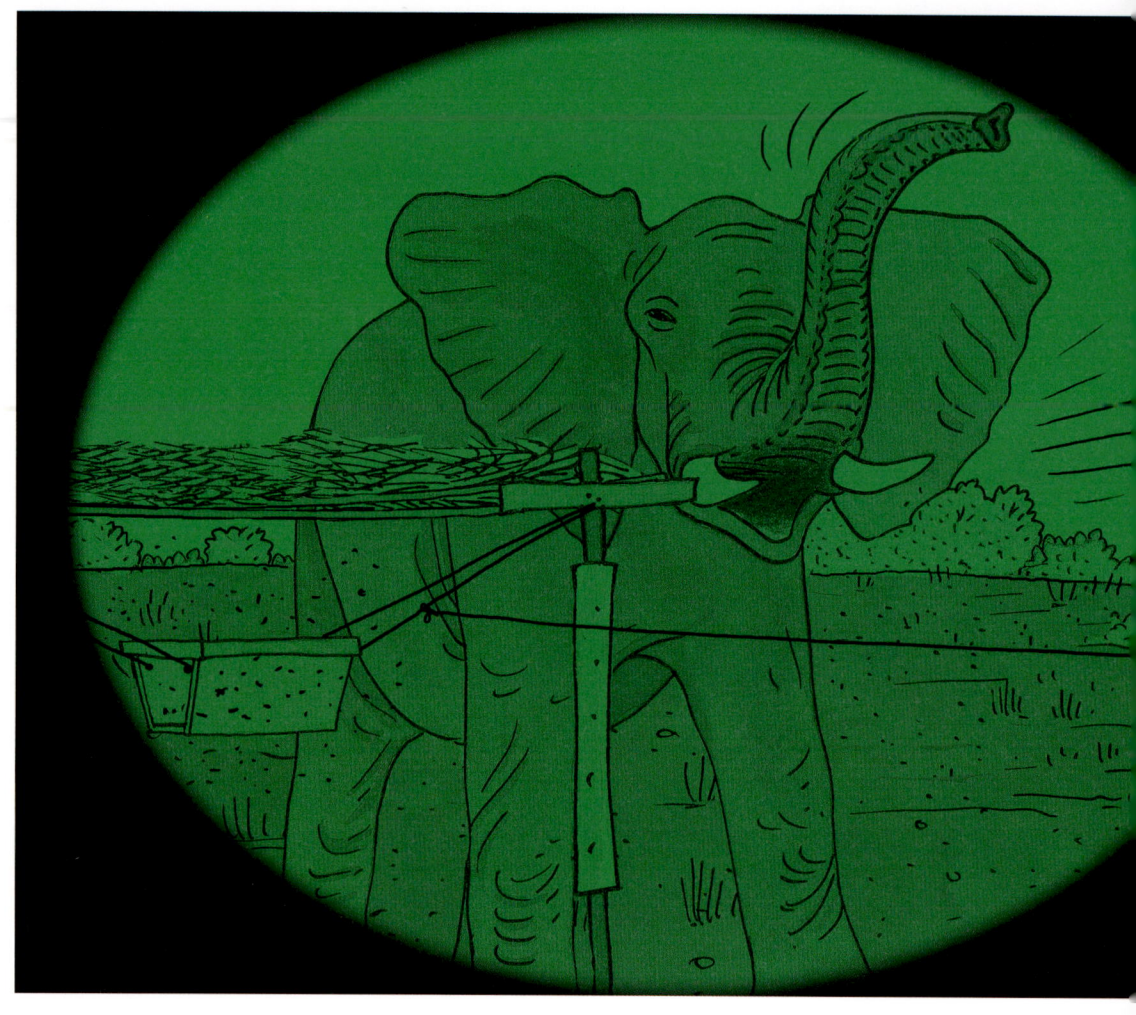

Then the female walked into the wire. This made the nearest hives swing and bounce. The bees in the hives buzzed angrily.

At once the elephants backed away. The large female raised her trunk and trumpeted.

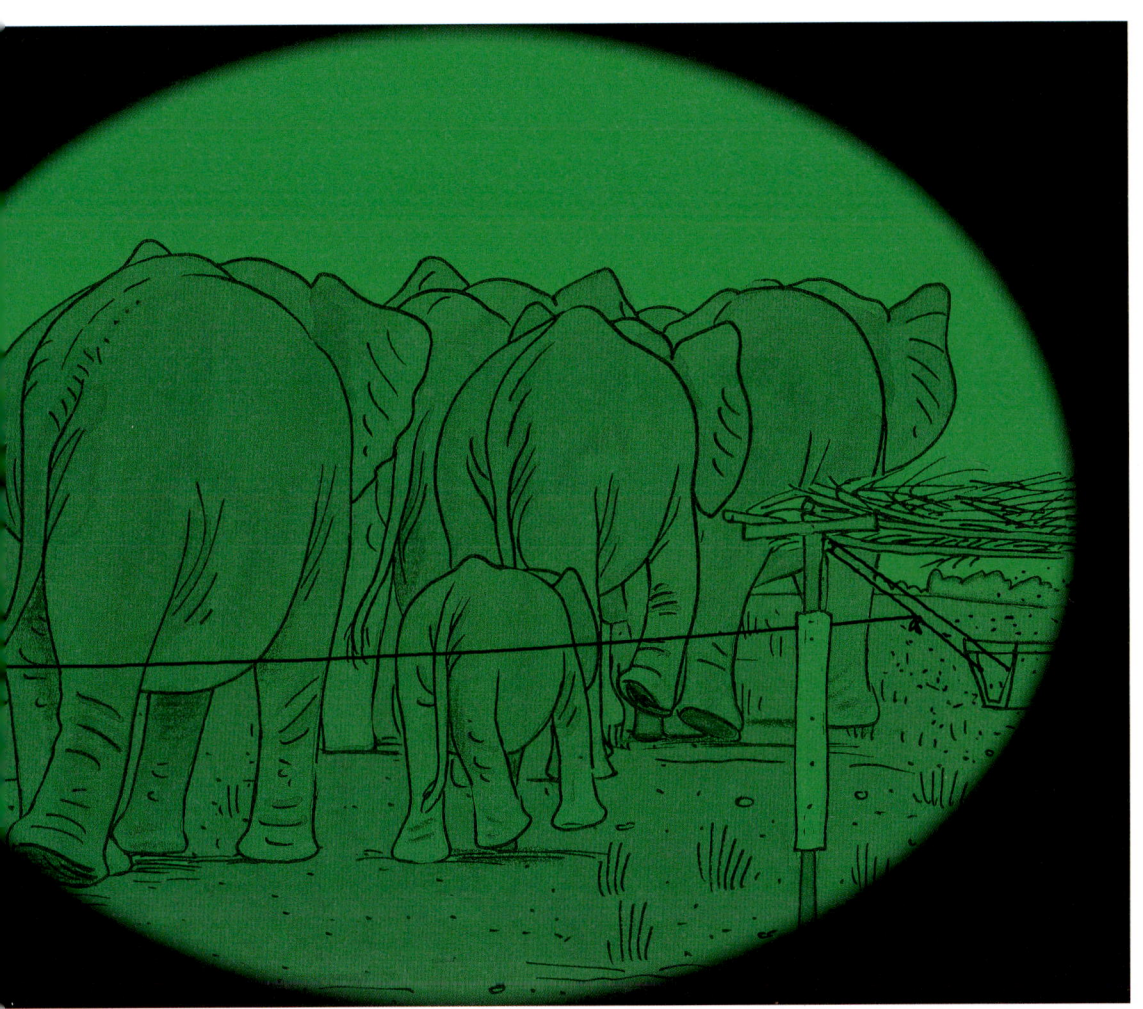

Then the herd turned and walked away into the darkness.

Biff was amazed. It was hard to believe that huge animals like these were scared of bees. Thanks to the bees, the villagers' crops had been saved.

"The beehive fence has worked," said Mukami,
excitedly. She gave Biff a little gift.

"I'm so glad," said Biff. She wanted to hug Mukami.
At that moment the key glowed.

Back at home, Biff took the bee suit off. She was no longer afraid of bees and she couldn't wait to tell Anneena about the adventure. She picked up a book and ran out to the tent.

"I know something about bees I bet you don't know," yawned Biff as soon as they were in bed.

"What's that?" asked Anneena.

But Biff didn't reply. She was so tired after putting up the beehive fence, she had fallen fast asleep.

Talk about the story

What did Anneena's dad tell Biff about bees?

Why did the villagers want the beehives?

Why did the beehive fence stop the elephants from raiding the crops?

What did you use to be afraid of? Have you overcome that fear?

Odd one out

Which pieces fit in the jigsaw puzzle?

Which is the odd one out?

Tips for reading *A Good Turn*

Children learn best when reading is relaxed and enjoyable.

- Talk about the title and the picture on page 42.
  Then read the speech bubble.

- Discuss what you think the story might be about.

- Encourage your child to read as much of the story as they can.

- Give lots of praise as your child reads, and help them
  when necessary.

- If your child gets stuck on a word that is decodable, encourage
  them to say the sounds and then blend them together to read the
  word. Read the whole sentence again. Focus on the meaning.

- If the word is not decodable, or is still too tricky, just read the
  word for them, re-read the sentence and move on.

- Where you can, use voices for different characters. Encourage
  your child to do the same. Reading with expression is fun.

- When you've finished reading the story, talk about it with your
  child, using the 'Talk about the story' questions at the end.
  Then do the activity.

Children enjoy re-reading stories, and this helps to build
their confidence.

Have fun!

For more activities, free eBooks
and practical advice to help
your child progress with reading
visit **oxfordowl.co.uk**

A Good Turn

Can Chip, Wilf and Nadim do a good turn when the magic key takes them to the very first Scout camp?

Chip had joined the Cub Scouts. Nadim was a leader of a patrol called a Six. They were playing a team game. They had to pick up blocks using an elastic band and four bits of string.

"We must all keep the tension the same," said Chip,
"so pull together."

The Cubs carefully placed their elastic band round
a block and picked it up.

They had to make a tower of six blocks. The first
team to build one was the winner.

Just as they were about to place the last block on their tower, it toppled over.

"Ah well, we came in last," said Nadim.

"It's taking part that counts," said Wilf, "but I still wanted to win."

The Cub pack leader, Akela, called the pack
together.

"Tonight is special," he said. "We are going to invest
Wilf and Chip and they are going to make their Cub
Scout Promise."

Chip and Wilf had learned the Promise off by heart, but Chip was still nervous in case he had forgotten it. They said it together. The Promise was about helping other people, and keeping the Cub Scout Law.

"What *is* the Cub Scout Law?" asked Dad.

"That's easy," said Chip. "Cub Scouts always do their best, think of others before themselves and do a good turn every day."

"Hmm!" said Dad. "A good turn, eh?"

"How about tidying your room?" said Dad. "That would be a good turn."

"No," said Chip. "I would only be helping myself. That wouldn't count."

"You could give us all a sweet," joked Wilf.

"That wouldn't count either," said Chip.

"Or Nadim could do this worksheet for me," said Kipper. "He is good at number facts."

"No," said Chip. "You wouldn't learn anything."

"Don't forget we promised Akela we'd find out more about the Scouts," said Wilf.

"Lord Baden-Powell set up the Scouts," said Nadim. "The first Scout camp was on Brownsea Island in 1907."

"That's a start. Let's find out more about Baden-Powell, too," said Wilf.

"Let's look on the Internet," said Chip.

The laptop was in Biff's room. It was on her bed with the magic key next to it.

Suddenly the key began to glow.

"The key might do us a good turn," said Chip, "and take us to meet Baden-Powell."

The magic took the boys back in time to Brownsea Island.

"See those tents," said Chip. "I bet this is the first Scout camp."

"Well," said Wilf, "if we do meet Baden-Powell, we won't be able to tell Akela."

"That must be a bell tent," said Nadim. "It has only one pole and it's in the middle."

"But where are Baden-Powell and all the boys?" asked Chip.

The tents were made of thick canvas. The boys could see a fire with a large cooking pot over it. Steam was curling up from the pot. Nearby was a table with plates and pots and pans on it. The camp looked deserted.

In one of the tents, three boys were peeling potatoes.
One of the boys came out and picked up a box of
carrots. He took them back inside.

"Let's leave them to it," said Chip. "They might make us help them peel the carrots."

"I suppose it would be our good turn if we did," laughed Wilf.

At that moment they heard voices in the distance.
They set off to find out where the voices were
coming from.

In a hollow, beyond some trees, they saw a group of
five boys all about thirteen years old. The boys were
arguing about something.

The boys had two poles and coils of rope but they all seemed puzzled.

When they saw Chip, Wilf and Nadim, one of them asked, "How did you get here? This island is private!"

"Er . . . are you doing a team exercise?" asked Nadim.

"Yeah," another boy said, "but we've no time to chat.
Mr Baden-Powell has set us a problem but we can't
solve it."

"What sort of problem?" asked Wilf.

"Between these planks is an imaginary river," the boy said. "We have to find a way to get over it. But these poles don't reach across. They're too short to make a bridge. We get points if we can cross the river without falling in."

Chip looked at Nadim. "You're good at solving problems," he said.

"Hmm . . . " said Nadim. "There may be a way to do it."

"What do you mean?" asked Wilf.

Nadim asked the boys to tie one pole horizontally so that it hung from the other.

"Now use the ropes to hold the first pole upright," he said.

Nadim stood on the horizontal pole and used his weight to make it swing in a circle.

"It could work!" shouted one of the boys. "You're
a genius!"

They placed the upright pole in the centre of the
imaginary river with the horizontal pole on the bank.
The first boy edged along the pole to reach the pole in
the middle.

He swung the horizontal pole round, then carefully moved along it to the opposite bank.

As each boy crossed the river, a rope was thrown to the other side to keep the middle pole steady.

The boys cheered when they were all across.

A man had been watching the exercise. As the last boy crossed, he called, "Well done, Ravens. You are the only patrol to do it!"

Chip nudged Nadim. "I think that's Lord Baden-Powell," he said.

The man frowned. He was about to ask Chip, Wilf and Nadim who they were, when a boy ran up in a panic.

"Alex has cut his finger chopping carrots," he panted. "We can't find the first-aid kit."

They ran to the camp. Baden-Powell looked in a
large tin chest.

"We've got a first-aid kit somewhere," he said.
"Where is it?"

Chip had some plasters in his pocket.

"It's not a deep cut," said Chip. "Put this plaster on it."

"Plaster! What is that?" said Alex.

"Cubs sometimes carry a simple first-aid kit," said Chip. "It is best to be prepared."

Baden-Powell looked up from the chest.

"How did you boys get to the island?" he asked.

But the key had glowed and Chip, Wilf and Nadim had vanished.

"Hmm! Be prepared?" he said.

"Well, we kept the Cub Scout Law. We did a good turn," said Nadim.

"But if we do a good turn on a magic adventure, we can't tell anyone," said Wilf thoughtfully.

Just then Biff and Wilma came in.

"We've been on an adventure and met Baden-Powell," said Chip. "Nadim solved a problem and I put a plaster on a cut finger. So we did two good turns."

"Putting a plaster on a cut isn't much of a good turn," said Biff.

"At least I *had* a plaster. I was prepared," said Chip.

"But if we do good turns on magic adventures and no one knows, do they count?" said Wilf.

"Of course," said Biff. "A good turn is a good turn."

"We found out lots about the Scouts and met Baden-Powell, but we didn't find out his first name," said Nadim.

"Easy," said Wilma. "It's Robert."

"I can think of a motto for magic adventures," laughed Chip. "Be prepared . . . for anything!"

Talk about the story

What was the problem the boys were trying to solve?

How did Nadim solve the problem?

Why didn't Alex know what a plaster was?

What good turns do you do?

Which one is Billy?

Try and spot a boy called Billy.

Billy has brown shorts. He wears a belt. He has a red tag on his shoulder.

He has a blue cap. There is a button missing on his shirt.

Tips for reading *What a Journey!*

Children learn best when reading is relaxed and enjoyable.

- Talk about the story and the picture on page 78.
  Then read the speech bubble.

- Discuss what you think the story might be about.

- Encourage your child to read as much of the story as they can.

- Give lots of praise as your child reads, and help them
  when necessary.

- If your child gets stuck on a word that is decodable, encourage
  them to say the sounds and then blend them together to read the
  word. Read the whole sentence again. Focus on the meaning.

- If the word is not decodable, or is still too tricky, just read the
  word for them, re-read the sentence and move on.

- Where you can, use voices for different characters. Encourage
  your child to do the same. Reading with expression is fun.

- When you've finished reading the story, talk about it with your
  child, using the 'Talk about the story' questions at the end.
  Then do the activity.

Children enjoy re-reading stories, and this helps to build
their confidence.

Have fun!

For more activities, free eBooks
and practical advice to help
your child progress with reading
visit **oxfordowl.co.uk**

What a Journey!

Mum and Dad take the family on a holiday by train, but the journey isn't quite what they expect!

It was an exciting time in the Robinson house. Floppy was going to stay with Gran. Mum and Dad were taking Biff, Chip and Kipper to an activity park.

The children were really looking forward to the week ahead.

"Have a lovely time," said Gran, as she drove off
with Floppy. "Send me a postcard."

"We won't have time," said Dad. "We'll send you
lots of photos."

"Bye! See you in a week," called Mum.

A taxi was coming to take the family to the
train station.

"Just make sure you've got everything," said Dad.
"I don't want you children moaning because you've
forgotten something."

"We won't," said Kipper.

"No, we've thought of everything," added Chip.

They arrived at the station in plenty of time.

Dad looked in his bag for the train tickets. Then he looked frantically in his pockets.

"Oh no!" he gasped. "I've left the tickets at home. They're on the kitchen table."

"You said you'd checked everything," sighed Mum.

At that moment, Mrs May drove up on her scooter.

"Hello," she said. "You all look worried. Is anything the matter?"

"We've left the train tickets at home," said Mum, "and it will take ages to go home in a taxi to get them."

"Right!" said Mrs May. She looked at Dad. "I'm meeting a friend but she's not due for ages. Hop on. I'll run you home. We can be back in ten minutes on the scooter."

"Good for Mrs May," said Biff.

"I'll see you . . . in ten . . . minutes . . ." called Dad, as the scooter zoomed off.

Nine minutes later, Dad was back. "Phew!" he said.
"That was some ride."

"Thanks, Mrs May," said Biff. "You're a star!"

"Dad's face is the same colour as the crash helmet
Mrs May gave him," whispered Chip.

"Come on!" said Mum. "Our train is in. Let's hope
nothing else goes wrong."

They found their seats on the train and soon they were on their way.

Mum and the children sat together. Dad settled down in his seat on the other side of the aisle.

"I'm looking forward to a nice relaxing journey," he said.

"I'm hungry," said Kipper. "Can we have our picnic now?"

"No," said Mum. "We'll have it later. We will be on this train for quite a long time, so just read your book or play a game."

"It's fun looking out of the window," said Chip.

A man was sitting next to Dad. He had fallen asleep. The train stopped at the next station with a jerk. The man woke up suddenly. He jumped up and rushed to get off.

"Sorry! Sorry!" said the man as Dad stood up to let him get by.

"Oh no!" said Dad. "That man has left his mobile
on the table. If I run, I may be able to catch him."

Dad picked up the mobile and hurried off the train
after the man.

"Be quick!" urged Mum. "The train doesn't stop
for long."

"Excuse me! Wait!" shouted Dad. "You left your mobile on the train."

"Goodness!" said the man. "Thank you so much. I'm glad you were getting off the train, too."

"No, I must get on again!" Dad turned to get back on the train, but it was moving off!

"Dad has been left behind," gasped Mum, as the train gathered speed. "Now what do we do?"

Chip waved frantically. "Run, Dad! Quick! Jump on!" he called.

"It's no good, Chip," said Mum. "Dad can't get on a moving train."

Luckily, Dad had his mobile in his pocket. He was able to call Mum at once.

"I'm sorry, everyone," he said. "I've got all the tickets, so get off at the next station. I'll be on the next train. You will have to join me on that one."

They got off at the next station to wait for Dad. Mum spoke to a lady at the information desk.

"Your next train stops here in an hour," the lady said. "There is one before that but it goes straight through and won't be stopping at this station."

"I hope Dad gets the right train," sighed Mum.

Half an hour later, a train whooshed by. Dad's startled face was at the window.

"Oh no!" cried Mum. "Dad is on the wrong train. He's gone past. Now what do we do?"

Mum phoned Dad. "It's your turn to get off now," she said. "Wait for our train and make sure it's the right one."

From their train, the children looked out for Dad.
Biff kept her fingers crossed that Dad would get it
right. In the end, Dad did get on and the family was
together again.

Biff gave Dad a hug. "I couldn't believe it when you
whizzed past us," she laughed.

"Nor could I," said Dad. "My heart sank!"

The train sped through the countryside. Then
suddenly it stopped. A long time went by. At last
they were told that a tree had fallen across the track.
The train could not go on. The ticket collector came
and said that everyone had to leave the train and go
on by bus.

To get to the buses they had to climb up a steep
embankment. Luckily, there was a narrow set of steps
and a team of people to help carry everyone's luggage.

"Well, if this is an activity holiday," puffed Mum,
"it has started early!"

They had a surprise when they saw the bus they had
to go on. It was quite an old one.

"It was a job getting enough buses at short notice,"
explained a lady. "We had to call every bus company
in the area. This one was also available so we had to
use it."

"It'll be fun riding in an old bus," said Kipper.

"Hop on," said the driver. "This bus rattles a bit, but she keeps going."

"Sounds a bit like Gran," joked Dad.

"Oh, Dad!" sighed Mum. "That was cheeky!"

The bus made a strange clanking noise as it started off.

They hadn't gone very far when the engine began to splutter and bang. There was a loud hiss and the bus stopped with a jolt.

"She's overheated," said the driver. "Sorry, folks. When the engine cools down, I'll put some water in the radiator. It will take time. You may have to wait for another bus."

"Goodness," exclaimed Mum. "This is getting to be quite a journey. Will we ever get there?"

Dad had made a call on his mobile. "I've phoned for a taxi," he said. "We can't wait any longer."

"Did you manage to get one?" asked Mum.

"Hmm! Not exactly a taxi," said Dad.

It was not a taxi. It was a stretch limo.

"For goodness' sake!" exclaimed Mum. "Why on earth did you order a stretch limo?"

"It's all I could get in a hurry," said Dad.

"Wow!" gasped Chip. "This is amazing."

"Why has a car been stretched?" asked Kipper.

The family finally arrived at the activity park. When they got out of the car some people took photographs of them.

"They think we are famous," laughed Biff.

"It's not every day I ride in a stretch limo," said Dad, " . . . or on a scooter . . . or an old bus . . ."

One of the staff offered to take all the luggage to their lodge in a trailer, towed by a buggy.

Dad had an idea. "Excuse me," he said. "May I ride in the buggy? I'm having a journey in lots of different forms of transport."

"Now what's Dad doing?" asked Biff.

"What a journey!" said Mum. "I thought we'd never get here."

"After supper we'll hire some bicycles," said Dad. "We'll need them. Our lodge is a long way from the centre and the activity park is really big."

"Fantastic!" said Kipper.

Once they had the bicycles, they cycled to the lake.

"Wow!" said Chip. "There's a zip wire across the water."

"There's only one thing for it," said Dad, "and it has to be done today. Hold my mobile, Biff."

Dad joined the queue of people waiting to go.

"Why is Dad going on the zip wire?" asked Kipper.

"I don't know," laughed Biff, "but I'm going to film this on his mobile."

"Yee-hah!" yelled Dad as he whizzed across the lake.

"Look at him now!" said Chip.

"Well, he's been whooshing past us all day," said Biff.

"He didn't shout 'Yee-hah' when he whooshed past on the train," said Chip.

Dad sat back and smiled. "Well, it's been a funny old day," he said.

Back at the lodge, Biff spoke to Dad. "Why were you so determined to go on the zip wire today?" she asked.

"Simple!" said Dad. "A zip wire is a form of transport. I wanted one more to add to my list."

"What do you mean?" asked Kipper.

"Work it out for yourself," laughed Dad.

"I don't know which was funnier," laughed Mum.
"You on Mrs May's scooter or you on the zip wire."
"I know which was scarier," said Dad.

Talk about the story

What was the first thing that went wrong? What went wrong after that?

What different types of transport did Dad use?

Why was Dad so determined to go on the zip wire?

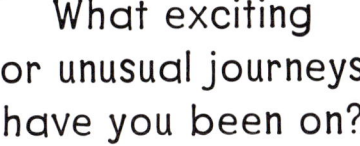

What exciting or unusual journeys have you been on?

Whose hats?

Which hat belongs to which character from the story? Look back through the story and check if you are right.

Tips for reading *The Fair-Haired Samurai*

Children learn best when reading is relaxed and enjoyable.

- Talk about the title and the picture on page 114. Read the speech bubble.

- Discuss what you think the story might be about. Aikido is a modern form of Japanese martial art.

- Encourage your child to read as much of the story as they can.

- Give lots of praise as your child reads, and help them when necessary.

- If your child gets stuck on a word that is decodable, encourage them to say the sounds and then blend them together to read the word. Read the whole sentence again. Focus on the meaning.

- If the word is not decodable, or is still too tricky, just read the word for them, re-read the sentence and move on.

- Where you can, use voices for different characters. Encourage your child to do the same. Reading with expression is fun.

- When you've finished reading the story, talk about it with your child, using the 'Talk about the story' questions at the end. Then do the activity.

Children enjoy re-reading stories, and this helps to build their confidence.

Have fun!

For more activities, free eBooks and practical advice to help your child progress with reading visit **oxfordowl.co.uk**

The Fair-Haired Samurai

Will Kipper's aikido classes come in useful when he has a magic key adventure in ancient Japan?

Kipper started going to aikido classes. He really
enjoyed it. The club met once a week in the school hall.
The teacher was Mr Otsuki but he told everyone to call
him Kenji.

"Aikido is a way of feeling," Kenji told them. "You don't need to be strong to defend yourself. Instead, you learn to turn other people's strength against them. Aikido shows you that strength comes from inside you."

Kenji taught the class to fall safely without hurting themselves. At first, it was quite hard to do but soon everyone could do a forward roll and land easily. As the weeks went by, the children got better and better at landing and rolling.

Kenji began to teach the class to do simple moves against a partner. The moves had Japanese names.

Kipper learned to grab his partner's arm and pull it back. He turned his body at the same time and his partner fell to the floor.

"We will learn the moves slowly at first," said Kenji. "The idea is to use your opponent's attack to your advantage."

Kipper worked hard in the classes.

"Excellent, Kipper," said Kenji. "Remember to bow. You must respect your opponent."

One day, Kipper decided to show Kenji the
photographs of the family holiday in Japan. The
photograph album was on Biff's bed. The key was lying
next to it.

As Kipper picked up the album, the key began
to glow.

"I don't want this," thought Kipper. "I want to get to my aikido class."

He flicked the key away and tried to run out of the room. The key landed just outside the bedroom door. But the magic took Kipper into the adventure anyway.

Kipper was on a high wall overlooking a Japanese castle. On one side of him he saw buildings and gardens. On the other side was a wall with a wide moat full of water.

The magic had taken him back in time to Nijo Castle in Kyoto in ancient Japan.

Kipper felt frightened. "I don't have the key," he thought. "How am I going to get back home without it? I might be here for ever. I wish I still had the key. I wish I hadn't been so impatient."

Kipper set off down a wide path lined with trees. Suddenly, he was confronted by a group of boys.

"Who are you? How dare you come in here! How did you get in?" they shouted.

"You are a spy!" the biggest boy shouted.

The boy ran to attack him. Kipper gasped. Then
he remembered Kenji's words, "Use your opponent's
strength against him."

He grabbed the boy's arm and turned sideways,
pushing his hip into the boy. The boy fell to the ground.

Another boy ran at him. Kipper jumped aside. He grabbed the boy's wrist and turned his shoulder. The speed of it made the boy somersault forward.

Kipper made a polite bow to his two opponents.

Then, a man appeared out of the trees. The boys
bowed low. Kipper gulped and did the same. The
biggest boy spoke.

"This boy with strange-looking clothes has entered
the castle and attacked us. He must be punished,
Mr Takeda," he said angrily.

"Ah, Isamu," the man said. "Your name means
courage. Is it brave to tell lies? It was you who attacked
first. I saw it all."

The man looked at Kipper. "Where did you learn
to defend yourself so well? Who are you? Why are you
here?" he asked.

Kipper gulped. He couldn't really tell them about the magic key. Then he remembered what Kenji had taught him about aikido.

"I am not strong," said Kipper, "but I have been taught that strength comes from inside you."

"Ha!" cried the man. "Did you hear that? Each one of you must understand that if you are to become a worthy samurai."

Mr Takeda took Kipper's arm.

"We will go to the Shogun's palace. He must see this boy who is so wise and resourceful," he said.

Kipper felt pleased that Mr Takeda had praised him.
He had remembered all that Kenji had taught him
and it had worked! He was glad he had learned aikido.
Kenji was right, he didn't have to be strong to overcome
a bigger opponent.

Mr Takeda had said the boys were to become samurai. Kipper knew that samurai were Japanese knights and they were strong and fearless.

Kipper felt nervous. He wondered what the Shogun would do with him.

"Bow low when you meet the Shogun and do not speak unless you are spoken to," Mr Takeda said sternly.

Mr Takeda told the Shogun what he had seen. The Shogun looked at Kipper and commanded him to come closer.

To Kipper's surprise, the Shogun laughed.

"So this fair-haired boy is clever enough to enter the castle, throw my two biggest sons, and is wise enough to impress you, Takeda. We must train him to be a samurai."

"It will please me to have a fair-haired samurai," the Shogun went on. He looked at Kipper. "The training is hard. It will take many years. It will test you to your limits. Do not fail or it will be the worse for you."

Kipper's heart sank.

At once, Kipper was sent to join the other boys.

"This is terrible," he thought.

He struggled to carry a large stone and place it on a wall. He had to race another boy to see who could get all the stones on the wall first.

The training went on all day. Kipper had to leapfrog
over the biggest boy. The boy was too tall and Kipper
fell to the ground. He had to try again and again.

"I don't want to be a samurai," thought Kipper.
"This is a lot harder than aikido."

At last it was supper time. Kipper was glad he knew
how to use chopsticks. The biggest boy asked where he
had learned to defend himself.

"Have you heard of aikido?" asked Kipper.

The boys shook their heads. They had never heard
of it.

After supper, it was bed time. Kipper was given a sleeping mat and a pillow made from a block of wood. He lay with the boys in a large room and they all fell asleep at once.

"I may be here for the rest of my life," he thought miserably.

At home, Floppy liked to sneak upstairs when no one was looking. He saw the key flashing faintly. He picked it up in his jaws and ran into Biff's room. As he did so, the key glowed and he was whisked through the door of the little house.

"Dogs don't have magic adventures by themselves, do they?" thought Floppy. But by now he was in the grounds of Nijo Castle. Floppy did what all dogs do. He began to sniff at the strange new smells.

Then he picked up a scent he knew!

Kipper couldn't sleep. He felt frightened and unhappy. This was the worst adventure he had been on. He was afraid he would never go home. A tear ran down his cheek and fell on to his wooden pillow.

Then he felt a wet nose press into his neck.

It was Floppy, holding the key firmly in his jaws. Kipper had to stop himself from shouting out loud.

"Floppy! You good dog," he whispered. "How did you know how to find me?"

The key began to glow.

Back in Biff's room, Kipper put the key back on
Biff's bed and patted Floppy on the head.

"I'm glad that adventure is over," he said. "I don't
think I would have been a very good samurai warrior.
I'd rather go to aikido classes!"

Dad called from downstairs. "Hurry up, Kipper.
You're going to be late for your aikido class."

Kipper picked up the photograph album and
then put it down again. He had something else to
show Kenji.

Before the aikido class began, Kipper showed Kenji
something.

"It looks like a very tiny wooden pillow. Wherever
did you get it?" asked Kenji.

Kipper gave a little smile. "Ah, I got it in Japan,"
he said.

Talk about the story

What was the main lesson Kipper learned from his aikido class?

Why didn't Kipper have the magic key with him?

Why did Kipper bow to the two boys who had attacked him?

Why is it good to have a sport or a hobby?

Word puzzles

Add one letter at a time to get from the top word to the bottom word in each pile of stones. Each letter must form a new word.

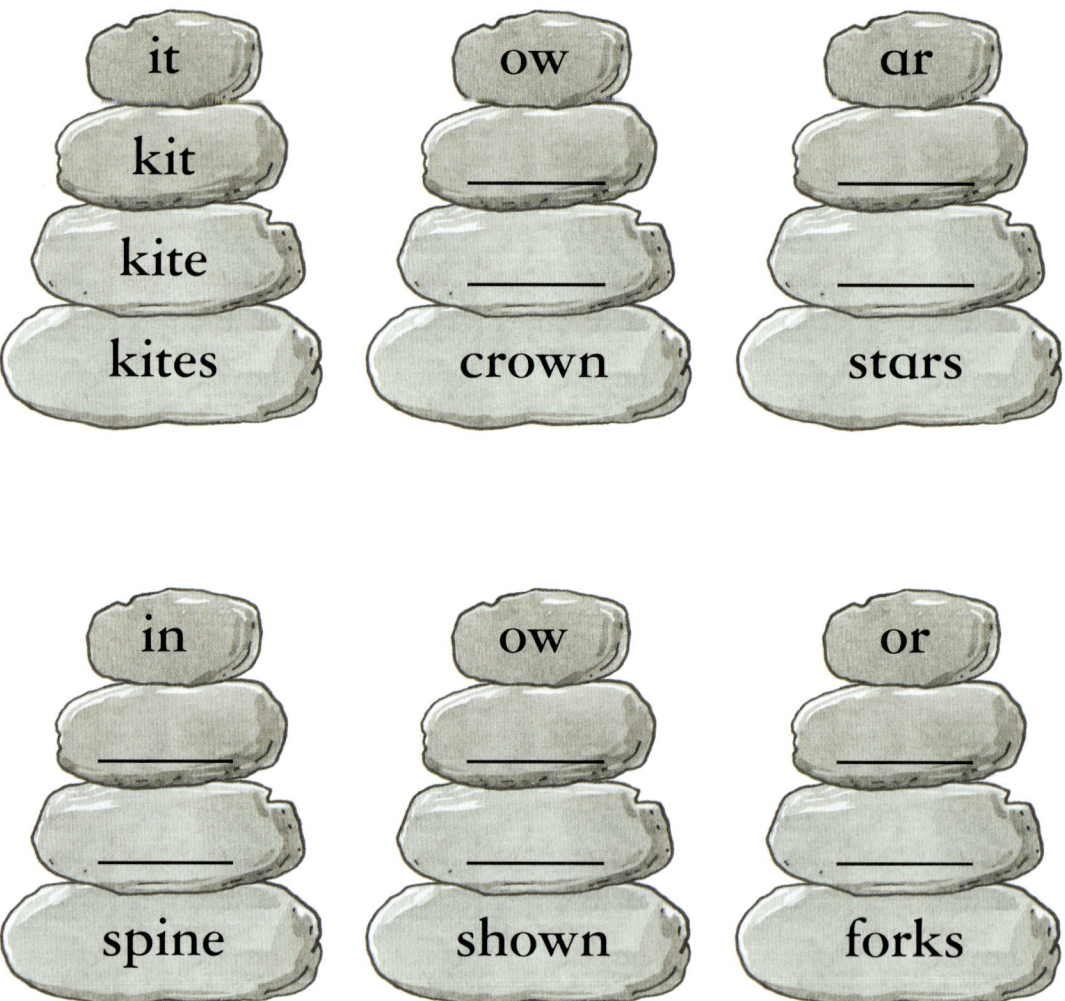

Remembering the stories together

Encourage your child to remember and retell the stories in this book. You could ask questions like these:

- Who are the characters?
- What happens at the beginning?
- What happens next?
- How does the story end?
- What was your favourite part? Why?

Story prompts

When talking to your child about the stories, you could use these more detailed reminders to help them remember the exact sequence of events. Turn the statements below into questions, so that your child can give you the answers. For example, *Where do the children sleep? What invades the garden?* And so on …

The Beehive Fence

- Biff and Anneena decide to sleep in a tent in Biff's garden.
- Biff is scared by a swarm of bees.
- The key takes Biff to Kenya where the villagers think Biff is the bee lady.
- Biff helps the bee lady to set up lots of beehives.
- The bees scare off elephants which have been eating crops.

A Good Turn

- Nadim, Wilf and Chip promise to find out more about the Scouts.
- The magic key begins to glow and takes them to the first Scout camp.
- Nadim helps some boys with their team exercise.
- When they get back home they explain how they met Baden-Powell.

What a Journey!

- The family is going to an activity park.

- Dad forgets the train tickets, so Mrs May takes him back on her scooter.

- They get on the train and then a man forgets his mobile phone!

- Dad tries to return the man's mobile phone to him on the platform, but the train leaves Dad behind.

- Dad catches up with the family, but they have to get a bus and then a limo to get to the activity park.

- They get to their lodge by buggy.

- Dad has had such an eventful day that he decides to go on the zip wire.

The Fair-Haired Samurai

- Kipper really enjoys going to aikido classes once a week.

- The magic key takes Kipper inside a Japanese castle, but he has left the key behind.

- Kipper uses aikido to defend himself when a bigger boy attacks him.

- An old man watches and says Kipper should be trained to become a samurai.

- The Shogun agrees. He is amazed by Kipper's fair hair. Kipper is unhappy.

- At home, Floppy sees the key flashing and is able to save Kipper.

You could now encourage your child to create a 'story map' of each story, drawing and colouring all the key parts of them. This will help them to identify the main elements of the stories and learn to create their own stories.